Perfect Health

OR

THE HIGHEST CURATIVE POWER IN MAN

BY

CHRISTIAN D. LARSON

Martino Publishing
Mansfield Centre, CT
2012

Martino Publishing
P.O. Box 373,
Mansfield Centre, CT 06250 USA

www.martinopublishing.com

ISBN   978-1-61427-306-6

© *2012 Martino Publishing*

Cover design by T. Matarazzo

Printed in the United States of America On 100% Acid-Free Paper

Perfect Health

OR

THE HIGHEST CURATIVE POWER IN MAN

BY

CHRISTIAN D. LARSON

L. N. FOWLER & CO.
7 Imperial Arcade, Ludgate Circus
LONDON, E. C.

1910
THE PROGRESS COMPANY
CHICAGO.

P. F. Pettibone & Co.
Printers and Binders
Chicago

BY THE SAME AUTHOR

Poise and Power . .	.50
Mastery of Fate . . .	.50
The Hidden Secret . .	.50
The Great Within . .	.50
Mastery of Self . .	.50
On The Heights . . .	.50
How Great Men Succeed .	.50
How to Stay Young . .	1.00
The Ideal Made Real . .	1.00
The Pathway of Roses .	1.50
Your Forces and How to Use Them	1.50

Published and For Sale by
THE PROGRESS COMPANY
CHICAGO.

Perfect Health

or

The Highest Curative Power in Man

HE principle upon which the higher form of healing is based is found in the statement that man is created in the image and likeness of God. The spiritual man is the real man, and the spiritual man is as God is—eternally perfect and whole through and through. To know this truth is to know the truth that makes man free, and this truth can be known by every mind that will enter into the conscious realization of the spirit of truth. The intellectual understanding does not produce the knowing of truth; to know the truth, the spiritual understanding becomes necessary. The intellectual understanding looks upon truth from without and thus

learns to comprehend the outer form of truth; the spiritual understanding enters into the very spirit of truth and thus gains the power, not only to know the truth itself, but also to know everything that exists within the wonderful world of truth.

There is a world of eternal truth where everything is as wonderful, as beautiful and as perfect as the truth itself; and there is a world of mere appearance where everything is passing, and where nothing is real. To live in the world of appearance is to pass through what seems to be real; to live in the world of truth is to dwell forever in that which is real. In the world of appearance we find pain, sickness, evil and death; and we must of necessity pass through those things so long as we continue to pass through the world of appearance. To continue to pass through the world of darkness is to continue to pass through the darkness itself. But in the world of truth, we find neither sickness nor pain, sorrow nor death; those things cannot exist in the world of truth; therefore, we shall be absolutely free from those things so long as we live in the world of truth. And to know the truth, that is, to enter into the consciousness of the spirit of truth, is to enter the world of truth.

To live in the world of truth is to live in the conscious possession of everything that exists in that world; and in that world everything is as perfect and as beautiful as when it first appeared from the creative hand divine. To live in the world of truth is to be free from those things that are not of the truth, and only those things are of the truth that are perfect as God is perfect. Therefore, in the world of truth there can be no sickness, because sickness is not perfect as God is perfect. Sickness can never enter the world of truth, but to enter the world of truth is to eliminate from the human system every trace of sickness that we ever thought we knew. Enter into the truth—into the very spirit of truth, and you are healed absolutely. You are every whit whole. Your emancipation is perfect and complete.

There are many ways to temporary health and limited degrees of freedom; but to enter the truth—the spirit of truth —the world of truth, is to gain that health that is as perfect and as endless as the truth itself, and that freedom that is as universal and as limitless as the truth itself. Therefore, we can find no better way to freedom, no higher path to health. To those who can understand, all other paths are useless, all other methods vain.

To follow other paths is to find but fragments; to enter the truth is to find the whole. The truth contains everything that is good for man; it is needless to seek elsewhere; but that which is not good for man cannot be found in the truth.

To enter into the truth the simple secret is to seek the spirit of truth. So long as we seek the mere mental form of truth, consciousness will dwell on the outside of truth; and no matter how much truth we may see, we shall continue to live in the world of untruth. But when we seek the spirit of truth—that divine something that exists within all truth, we enter consciously into the truth, and will therefore be filled and surrounded by the life of truth. We shall, accordingly, live the truth, and to live the truth is to give to life everything that is contained in the truth. Everything that pertains to the true being of man is thus expressed in every element throughout the entire being of man; and as perfect health is eternal in the true being of man, perfect health will likewise become eternal in every part of man. So long as we live the truth, that is, live consciously in the world of truth, not a fibre in the physical body can ever be sick, and not a single adverse mental condition can exist within us for a moment.

We are conscious in every atom in the body, and what enters into consciousness will therefore enter into every atom in the body. When we are in the spirit of truth we are conscious of absolute health; absolute health will thus enter into our consciousness—into every part of our consciousness, which means that absolute health will enter into every atom in the body, because consciousness extends to every atom in the body. To be conscious of absolute health is to possess and express absolute health in every part of consciousness, and accordingly, in every part of the body, for every part of the body exists within the field of consciousness. In like manner, to live the truth is to live the truth in every atom in the body, and thus give, to every atom in the body, the elements of true being, one of which is absolute health. We conclude, therefore, that so long as we are in the truth and are conscious of true being, it is not necessary to give thought to the body. And what is more, to think of the body as being distinct from true being is to hinder the mind from gaining complete consciousness of true being.

To think of true being as being one part of man and the physical body as being the other part, is to recognize two distinct entities in man, one of which is perfect and the other of which is imperfect; but no house that is divided against itself can stand; therefore, so long as we think of the physical body as being a separate and imperfect entity, we are not in the truth, and ills in abundance will appear in the personal life. In the truth there is no thought of imperfection and no thought of separation. In the truth, the being of man is one, and that one is perfect. The physical body is not looked upon as a thing apart, or as a something that can get sick; but is looked upon as a reflection of divine being, and is therefore thought of as having the same perfection as divine being.

The real man is well, always was and always will be, because the real man is created in the image of God. But the body is not separated from the real man; the body is a reflection of the real and is therefore similar to the real man in all things. If the body seems to be imperfect the cause is found in the mind which is the mirror. When the reflection differs from that which is reflected, the mirror does not reflect properly; and the remedy lies, not in trying to modify the reflection, but in trying to remove the defects from the mirror. Do something to make the mirror reflect properly and the reflection will be the exact likeness of that reality that is being reflected. And here we find the secret to the highest healing—the complete emancipation of man.

The true being of man is perfect, and the mind is the mirror reflecting the perfection of true being. This reflection appears in the form of the visible personality, but it may not always appear in the exact likeness of true being. When the personality does not manifest the qualities of true being, we try to change the personality; we try to modify personal conditions by acting upon those conditions themselves, regardless of the cause of those conditions; in brief, we try to "doctor" the effect while permitting the cause to remain undisturbed. The result is a number of confused systems of healing, all of which aim to give relief or emancipation, but none of which can remove the cause. The only good they can possibly do is to stay the actions of the effects temporarily so that man may have occasional periods of peace. Beyond this they can not go; therefore, man will not find real emancipation until he learns how to remove the cause; and the cause is to be found in the mirror. Remove the defects from the mirror and the reflection will

be the exact likeness of the reality standing before the mirror. When the mind
properly reflects the real man, the personal man will express the perfection of
true being; the personal in man will manifest the real in man, and the real in man
is created in the image of God.

E HAVE three factors to consider; viz., the real man, the mirror and the reflection, otherwise termed the visible personality. The real man is always well, and lives perpetually in complete emancipation; therefore, the personal man, being a direct reflection of the real man, should also have perpetual health and emancipation. But this is not always so, and the reason why is that the mind—the mirror —does not properly reflect the real man. If the mind was so constructed that it would reflect perfectly the true being of man, the personal man would always be as perfect, as wholesome and as divine as the real man, and neither sickness nor weakness nor any evil whatever could possibly exist in the personal life of man any more. His life would be from above, and from above only, and his emancipation would be complete.

When the mind knows the truth, and actually lives in the consciousness of the spirit of truth, it becomes a perfect mirror and, in consequence, will perfectly reflect the true being of man. The defects in the mirror are composed simply of beliefs that are untrue; these beliefs turn aside some of the rays of light from the divine spirit within, and the reflection is distorted. Thus we have imperfect conditions in the personality. When all false beliefs are removed from the mind, there are no defects any more in the mirror, and the reflection will be perfect. To remove false beliefs from the mind, the simple secret is to enter the truth—the spirit of truth. To know the truth is to make the mental mirror clean and thus cause every ray of divine light to be reflected fully and perfectly. The life, the health, the purity, the power and the wisdom of the within will thus appear in personal form in the without.

We know the truth when our minds reflect the truth; that is what it means to know the truth; but our minds will not properly reflect the truth unless the mental mirror is clean. Perfection means full expression, and the personal man will be a full expression of the true being of man when the mental mirror is so clean that all of true being is reflected. However, when there are "spots" on the mirror, the reflection will not be complete; some of the rays of the spirit within will be lacking, and it is this lack that constitutes the original cause of every ill that appears in personal existence. When every atom in the personality is full with life and wholeness from within, there can be neither disease nor weakness in any part of the physical body; and this fullness invariably appears in the personality when the mind reflects the whole of true being. When the mirror reflects perfectly, the reflection will manifest everything that exists in that which is being reflected. Nothing will be lacking, and that which appears will be just as perfect, just as beautiful and just as true as that which is. The seeming will be the exact likeness of the real, but these two will be one. The reflection does not exist apart from the real, therefore we must never think of the reflection as real. We must never think of the body as real; it is simply a reflection of the real; and when the mental mirror reflects properly, the physical reflection will be just as beautiful and just as wholesome as the spiritual reality.

When the true being of man is perfectly reflected in personal existence, the Word becomes flesh, and the tangible elements of the body become external pictures of the divine idea within—the spiritual idea of absolute truth. Accordingly, materiality, grossness and physical ills must disappear, because those conditions are simply the results of confused reflections. When the mind reflects the wholeness of the spirit, the body becomes as pure, as clean, as refined and as beautiful as the spirit; and likewise, as strong as the spirit. The life, the power and the divinity that is within will manifest in the without, and as the spiritual man is, so will the visible man be also.

To try to heal the body is therefore not only unnecessary, but is actually an obstacle in the way of healing. Emancipation comes to the body only when the fullness of the spirit of truth finds expression in the body, but before the body can receive the expression of truth the mind must know the spirit of truth. The reflection becomes true to the real when the mirror becomes true to its own function. When the mental mirror reflects the perfection of true being the body will express, in every atom, the perfection of true being. But so long as we are trying to heal the body by simply dealing with effects as we find them in the body, we will not give our attention to those causes that exist beyond the body. So long as we devote all our efforts towards trying to remove defects from the reflection, we will do nothing to remove defects from the mirror. It is the defects in the mirror that cause the defects in the reflection; it is untrue states in the mind that produce untrue conditions in the body; therefore, no attention need be given to the healing of the body; such efforts will profit nothing. Do not think of the body, because it is only a reflection and not a reality; give your attention to the mind; make the mental mirror clean; remove the false and the foreign from its surface so that it may become perfectly clear in every part. And you do this by immersing the mental mirror in the crystal waters of the spirit of truth. In brief, enter the spirit of truth, and your mind will become as pure as the spirit of truth. Thus you may clearly see and perfectly know the truth; all your thoughts will reflect the truth, and your visible being will be the expression of truth. Outer being will become a true reflection of true being, and you will realize in personal existence what you have learned to know in spiritual existence.

What we think of as disease is simply a broken reflection, and not a reality in itself. But this broken reflection cannot be reset; it must be removed completely and give place to a true reflection; and the true reflection appears when the mirror is made clean. The reason why the mental mirror is not always clean is found in the fact that the mind can be impressed from without. Everything that enters through the senses will impress the mind, and if consciousness is not selective, many impressions will be formed that are not in accord with absolute truth. Such impressions will become "foreign material," as it were, upon the glass of the mirror, and will hinder true reflection. But we must not close the mind to the world of sense; we are here to manifest the real, and to do so the within must act upon the without; we must be conscious of the without and susceptible to all that is taking place in the external world. However, we should look upon life, not from the view point of the valley, but from the view point of the mountain top.

When we look upon life through the limitations of the personal vision, we do not see things as they are, and accordingly those impressions that come from without are not true; but when we look upon life through the vision of the spirit and from the heights of absolute truth, we see all things as they are; the mind is thus impressed with the truth, both from within and from without. No "foreign material" is permitted to gather upon the mirror because all the impressions that enter the mind are rays from the omnipresent light of universal truth; and rays of light will not produce "spots" upon any mirror. When we see all things as they are, the mind receives nothing but truth from any source. We can open the mind fully to the world of physical sense as well as the world of spiritual sense; only rays from the light of truth will come upon the mental mirror; and that mirror will reflect only the truth through every part of body, mind and soul.

To reduce physical substance to its last analysis is to discover that the physical body is not solid. It appears to be solid, because those elements of which it is composed vibrate at a rate that produces a sensation that we interpret as tangible; and that sensation serves a true purpose in our present sphere of existence, but the sensation of a thing and the thing itself are not the same. When we think of the body as solid we not only school ourselves to believe that the physical can only with difficulty be changed or modified by the mind, but we also form the habit of viewing the body as "material." And whenever we think of anything as "material" we cause "materiality" to gather over the glass of the mental mirror. Thus we hinder the true reflection of perfect being, and bring upon ourselves conditions that are incomplete, misdirected, adverse, imperfect and untrue. But when we think of the body, not as solid matter, but as spirit made visible, every thought that we form of the body will be a spiritual thought, and such thoughts invariably convey the health, the wholeness, the power and the life of the spirit.

When we realize that all physical conditions are reflections of mental states, and realize that we can create all our mental states in the exact likeness of absolute truth, we elevate the mind to the lofty position of absolute supremacy over the body. We take our place as complete masters of our own personalities and everything that personal existence may contain; and when we place ourselves in the position of mastership we begin to exercise mastership. He who realizes that he is master of his life, will gain the power to master his life. When we know that all physical conditions are reflections from the mental mirror within, we are no longer in bondage to conditions; we know that we can reflect what we like, and therefore produce any physical condition that we like. Simply to know this great truth is to take the mind out of bondage into freedom, and when the mind is free from adverse conditions the body will be free from those conditions also. The mind that is free from adverse conditions will not reflect such conditions; and your mind becomes absolutely free from all conditions the moment you realize or inwardly know that you can reflect any condition that you may desire.

When you know that you can walk you are not in bondage to the thought that you can not walk, because there can be no such thought in your mind. Likewise, when you know that you can fill your body with the power of absolute health, you are no longer in bondage to disease. When you know that you have the power to do what you wish to do, it is not possible for you to think that you do not have that power. You cannot feel the absence of something when you feel the presence of that something. When you know that you are true being, it is not possible for you to think that there is anything wrong or untrue in your being; and so long as you do not think that there is anything wrong in your being, no wrong can possibly exist in your being. To think the whole truth is to reflect the whole truth, and when the whole

truth is reflected in your life there will
not be any room for false conditions in
your life. You will be perfect and whole
through and through.

When you realize that your true being
is perfect and whole in all things, and that
your visible personality is simply a reflection of what you think of your true being,
your attitude towards both the without
and the within is in perfect accord with
absolute truth. You have placed yourself in perfect harmony with the true
order of things, physically, mentally and
spiritually, and you may henceforth give
full expression to the true in every part of
your being. You realize that your personality is completely in your own hands,
because he who controls the source of
light may determine the measure of light
that is to be given. All obstacles to a
complete mastery of the outer life has
been removed through your realization
of the great truth that you can bring
forth any measure desired of the inner
life. And you find that your greatest
purpose is to gain a more and more perfect realization of true being so that you
can reflect in the personal man all that
has existence in the wholeness, the perfection and the divinity of the real man.

HEN we learn that imperfect conditions in the body are produced by broken, distorted or interrupted reflections from within, and that "foreign material" on the mental mirror is the cause of such reflections, we may conclude that the cause of every disease is in the mind, or that it is the mind that is sick instead of the body; but such thoughts or conclusions must never be permitted. The mirror is not defective simply because there is "foreign material" upon its surface; the mirror itself is perfect if it was made right in the first place; likewise, the mind in itself is perfect regardless of the fact that it may contain impressions that are not true. Every mind is formed in the likeness of Divine Mind; every human mind is created right in the beginning and no power can cause that which is right to become wrong; therefore, the human mind is always right, always perfect, always well. Never think of your mind as being sick; the mind can never become sick; sickness can never enter that which is originally and permanently perfect. And never think

of your mind as being the cause of disease, or as containing the cause of disease. Perfection can neither be the cause of imperfection nor contain such a cause; and the human mind is, in itself, perfect, being created in the image of Divine Mind.

The real man is well, and the real man is all there is in the human entity; therefore, you can never truthfully say that you are sick; the real mind can never be sick, nor can the unreal mind be sick because the unreal does not exist; the same is true of the body; that which is real in the body is a perfect reflection of the real man within, and that which does not reflect the real is unreal, or without existence whatever. The soul can not be sick because it is created in the image of God; the mind can not be sick because it is an expression of the mind of God—an individualized ray of light proceeding eternally from the Supreme Light; and the body can not be sick because it reflects in the visible a portion of the divinity of being that exists in the invisible. There is nothing in you that can be sick; all that is real in you is as God is, and God is never sick. All that is real in any sphere of existence is perfect in that sphere, and that which is perfect can not be sick. We cannot separate existence from reality, nor can we separate reality from perfection; and to be perfect in any part of the scale of life is to be true to life in that scale. But nothing that is true to life in any scale can be sick while in that scale. To be true to life is to be well, and all that is real in life is true to life.

What we think of disease need not concern us in the least; we cannot produce light by trying to analyze darkness; nor can we produce harmony by trying to understand the nature of discord. All study of imperfection is useless; in fact, more than useless, because the further we delve into the darkness of the false the further we depart from the light of truth. The laws of growth are not discovered through a study of emptiness, nor can we produce health, which is the fullness of life, by acting upon disease, which is the absence of life. To try to modify the effect will not change the cause, nor will a study of effect lead to an understanding of cause. From the view-point of absolute truth we know that disease is unreal and that it does not belong to the real nature of man. What the unreality of disease may consist of is of no importance whatever; first, because we do not care to know disease; and second, because the more we study disease or think of disease, the less we shall know of health. Besides, we can never know that which is not real; we can form mental pictures of the unreal but that is all; that which is not a thing in itself the mind can never know, and every attempt to understand that which is "not a thing" leads to the formation of confused mental pictures. Such pictures invariably "cloud" the mental mirror so that the real man is not properly reflected. In consequence, to try to understand disease is to produce more disease, and to try to analyze the nature of that which is not real is to prevent the full expression of that which is real.

To understand the fullness—the greater and greater fullness of that which is real, is the purpose of the mind. The more we grow into the consciousness of the real the clearer becomes the mental mirror, and the more perfectly the health, the power and the life of the real man is reflected in the personal man. To know the truth is to secure perfect freedom, but we do not actually know the truth so long as we also attempt to know the untruth. We are fully conscious of the real only when we are fully unconscious of the unreal, and we begin to understand absolute truth only when we cease to recognize anything but that which is absolute truth or the direct product of absolute truth. The eye must be single upon The Truth, and wherever we direct attention we should attempt to see The Truth as the soul, the life, the foundation, the substance, the being, the reality of everything. Your mind will never be impressed by that which seems imperfect in anything when your sole purpose is to see the true and the perfect in everything. You thus cause the mental mirror to remain perfectly clear and clean, and only the true in the spirit within is reflected and expressed in the form without.

That man is created in the image of God is the basic principle; and since God is absolute health, man must be absolute health also. When man realizes that he is always well in his true being, and that his true being is all of his being, he becomes conscious of absolute health. Whatever we become conscious of we give to every atom in our being, because we are conscious in every atom; and therefore, to be conscious of absolute health is to realize, possess and live absolute health in every atom. To gain and retain the consciousness of absolute health it is necessary to grow in the consciousness of absolute health; and this growth in consciousness is promoted, first, by thinking the truth about true being; second, by thinking only of true being, and third, by thinking that true being is all of being. When these three essentials are fully complied with, every thought will be formed in the likeness of the truth, will contain the truth, will be the truth; and as the mind moves into that which we think of the most, we shall accordingly move more and more into the truth, and into the consciousness of everything that is in the truth. Perfect health is in the truth, and therefore, we will, in this manner, grow more and more in perfect health, gaining higher degrees of health as well as greater degrees of physical, mental and spiritual strength. That it is necessary to grow in health in order to retain health, is evidenced by the fact that consciousness cannot remain at a standstill. When we do not rise into the greater we fall back into the lesser, and we will continue to lose ground steadily. But when we continue unceasingly to grow into the greater we not only retain all that we have gained thus far, but we also add to this an ever growing measure.

To grow into any quality or superior state of being, it is necessary to grow in the consciousness of the truth of that state of quality. We grow into health as we become conscious, more and more, of the truth about health—the absolute truth about perfect health. The truth is the soul of real being, and it is only as we enter into the truth of real being that we become conscious of that which is contained in real being. The same is true of any state or quality; we must know the truth that is in that state, and in that knowing grow perpetually. The truth that is in health is the truth that real being now does possess, and ever will possess, perfect health. Know the truth that you are in perfect health; that you will always remain in perfect health, because the real man is forever well as God is forever well, and the real of you is all of you; then grow in that truth; become more and more conscious of the very spirit of that truth, and the limitless life of the health within you will express itself more and more in the person without. In brief, you will actually live in an ever-growing measure of health, and to live in health is to possess health, through and through, in every atom that is alive, which means every atom in your own domain, because every atom is alive. To live in the consciousness of any quality is to give the fullness of that quality to every part of being, physical, mental and spiritual; and we always live in the consciousness of health when we inwardly know that real being actually is health. Real being and perfect health can not be separated; the two are absolutely and eternally one; and you are real being; therefore, you, yourself, are perfect health; the fact that you are alive proves that you are well; in real being, to be alive is to be well; health and life are one in the truth, and the whole of you is in the truth; the whole of you is composed of absolute truth, and the whole of you will eternally abide in the very spirit of absolute truth.

Realize what you are in the divinity of your being. This is the secret. Realize that you are well through and through, because you are well through and through, and you will be conscious only of perfect health. To gain and develop this realization, consciousness must ascend into the true state of being; and consciousness will ascend into the true —will enter into the very life of the true, as we train all the actions of mind to move towards the true. Keep the eye single upon the wholeness of divine being; know that you are in the wholeness of divine being because you are divine being, and desire to enter more and more deeply into that wholeness; then give conscious recognition to absolute wholeness in every thought, feeling and state of mind. You thus inspire everything in your being to ascend in the truth of real being, and, in consequence, every mental action will choose absolute truth as its goal. But such a goal is not for the future alone to reach; the very moment we begin to move towards absolute truth we begin to realize truth; and with the realization of truth comes the possession of all those superior qualities that exist within the world of truth. Among those we find perfect health, the life more abundant, the peace that passeth understanding, the joy everlasting and the power that cannot be measured.

O ENTER completely into the realization of your divine being, have faith in everything that is real and true. Have faith, not simply in that which seems greater than you, but have faith in that divine greatness that actually is you. To have faith is to enter into that in which we express faith, and it is the entering into the true, the perfect and the divine that produces complete emancipation. Faith, therefore, becomes an indispensable factor in the realization of truth. To affirm truth, or to train the mind to habitually think in the exact language of truth is not sufficient; we do not actually think the truth unless we think in the spirit of truth, and it is only through the attitude of faith that the mind can enter the spirit. Without faith, thinking is purely intellectual; but the intellectual understanding of truth does not produce the knowing of truth; we know the truth only when we enter into the spirit of truth, and it is only faith that has the power to enter into the spirit. When the intellect is inspired by faith, all under-

standing becomes spiritual; the mind no longer looks at the outer form of truth, but enters completely into the real life of truth, and it is when we are actually IN the truth that we know the truth.

To have faith, aim to enter into the inner life of everything of which you are conscious, or to which you give your thought. When you see anything or think of anything, do not simply recognize the outer form; know that there is an inner life, a spiritual life, within the form, and give that inner life your fullest recognition. Whatever you desire, enter mentally into the spirit of the action of that desire; try to feel the power of that limitless force that is within the soul of your desire, and realize that this supreme power can, and will, cause your desire to come true. Whatever you will to do, use the spirit of the will and not simply the external form of the will; recognize an inner power in the will, and will to will with this inner power. The inner power of the will is divine will, and to consciously use divine will is to CONNECT your will with the will of God. You will, in consequence, realize your purpose, because the will of God not only can do all things, but will do all things that we desire to have done. When you combine your will with Infinite will you invariably gain what you have in view; your will becomes strong enough to accomplish anything; and whenever you enter into the spirit of your own will, you find yourself in possession of the power of divine will. Faith is the secret. To enter into the spirit of anything is to exercise faith, and the more we try to enter into the spirit of everything the more we develop the power of faith. Remove the idea that faith means belief; faith is not to believe something but to do something; faith is not a passive conviction, but a positive action; faith does not rest serenely in the acceptance of some thought, but actually enters into the greater power and the greater life that is found in the vast spiritual domains of that thought.

When you proceed to heal yourself, enter mentally into the spirit of your true being; and when you realize that you are in a more spiritual state of being, proceed to enter into the spirit that is within that spiritual state. You thus gain conscious realization of the spirit within the spirit; your life is deepened, your mind is heightened, and your consciousness of the divine perfection of your true being is perpetually enlarged. It is growth in the spirit that produces complete emancipation, and to continue in this growth we must realize that every spiritual state has within itself a higher spiritual state. However deeply we may enter into the spirit, there is always a deeper spiritual state within the state we have realized; and however high we may ascend in the spiritual scale there is always a higher spiritual world before us. There are spiritual states within spiritual states without end, and there are spiritual worlds above spiritual worlds without end; therefore, to enter into the spirit of anything is not to enter into some final state that exists within the form; to enter into the spirit is to enter the realization of the real and begin an endless path in the realization of the greater and the greater that is contained within the limitless world of the real. The spirit of everything is the real of everything, and the more deeply we enter the real of anything the more perfectly we realize the spiritual life of that truth that is the very soul of everything. To realize that spiritual life is to gain complete emancipation, because to be in the spirit is to be IN the truth, and when we are in the truth we are in those things only that are perfect and good as pure truth is perfect and good.

To enter into the spirit of your true being is to begin to live in the real life of your true being; you live no longer in the confused world of mental pictures, but you live in the calm, illumined world of truth; and in the world of truth there is neither sickness, weakness, evil or wrong; to be in the world of truth is to be free; and we enter the world of truth when we know the truth, that is, when we consciously enter into the spirit of truth. When we are in the spirit of truth the mind will not be impressed by that which is untruth; the eye does not come in contact with darkness when it is in the light; in consequence, the mental mirror will be perfectly clear and clean, and will reflect in the person the full glory of that light that is in the spirit. The wholeness of the real man within will thus appear in the visible man without, and we shall find the same purity, health and strength in the body that we find in the perfection of divine spirit. The reflected ray contains the same elements as the original light from which it proceeds, providing the mirror reflects properly; and the mental mirror will reflect properly when its surface is covered with nothing but the brilliancy of divine truth. We conclude, therefore, that so long as you mentally live in the spirit of truth your mind will reflect only that which is in the truth; and as all physical conditions are but reflections from the mind, you will possess only wholesome physical conditions, because there are no unwholesome conditions in the truth. When the mind is in the truth it reflects only what is in the truth; the body will thus be filled, through and through, with perfect health; the personal man will express the strength, the life and the purity of the real man, and all that is beautiful and ideal in the within will manifest itself more and more in the without. When there is anything that you wish to gain or realize, be it in your own personality or in your environment, enter into the spirit of it; try to place yourself in mental touch with the inner life of the thing desired, and while you are giving recognition to that inner life, desire and pray for what you want with all the power of spirit and soul. Enter into the spirit of health when you pray for health; enter into the spirit of your being when you affirm that you are well, and you will not only gain what you desire, but you will also increase your faith, thus preparing yourself for the gain and the realization of greater things in the near future. To place the mind in contact with the inner life or the spirit of the thing desired will awaken the greater power of the mind—the real, soul power of the mind; and as that power is the coming forth of Supreme power in you, your life is placed in a position where nothing can be impossible. This is how all things become possible through faith. To have faith is to enter the spirit of things, and to enter the spirit is to enter the power of the spirit—the power of the Supreme— that power that can do anything no matter what the circumstances may be. All things become possible to him who has faith because faith CONNECTS the life of man with the life and power of the Most High.

To apply the principle of faith in the realization of perfect health, enter into the spirit of perfect health whenever you think of health. Aim to live in the soul of health, or what may be termed the real, interior life of health. This attitude will bring forth more and more of the power of health until your entire personality is entirely full of this power. You will thus not only realize the fullness of perfect health, but also the vital strength of health; and you will put to flight that erroneous idea that an increase of spiritual power means a decrease of physical power. Real spirituality produces strength, vigor and power on all planes —physical, mental and spiritual. Real spirituality, however, is not based upon emotionalism or negative goodness, but upon the consciousness of absolute truth. To be conscious of absolute truth is to express the life, the health and the power of absolute truth in every part of body, mind and soul; and the power of truth is not limited; therefore, the more we grow in the consciousness of truth the stronger we shall become throughout our entire being. The belief that the soul can, under certain conditions, be stronger than the body has no foundation in truth. When the soul seems to be strong and the body weak, the soul is not properly expressed in the body, and the fault lies in the mental mirror. When you feel a great deal of spiritual strength, you will reflect and express that strength in the body, providing you have a clear understanding of the true nature of that strength. But when the understanding is not clear the mental mirror will not reflect properly, and the strength of the spirit will not come forth to give strength to the body. The remedy is to know the truth—to enter into the spirit of truth, and to know that to be IN the truth is to be filled, through and through, with the limitless power of truth.

PIRITUALIZE your personality at all times, especially when you undertake to remove some ailment. Spiritualize your entire personality by realizing, through your mental vision, that every atom in your being is pure spirit—as pure and as clear as crystal, and as highly refined as the most sublimated essence of the soul. Spiritualize any part of your body, in the same manner, if that part is ailing, and imperfect conditions will begin at once to disappear. Realize the spiritual perfection and the divine wholeness of every part of your personality; spiritually see the divine counterpart of any part wherein you wish to realize perfect health, and know that the divine counterpart is the all of that part. Know that the physical is simply a reflection of your consciousness of the divine, and that this reflection will become stronger and more perfect as your consciousness of the divine becomes more perfect. When your consciousness of the divine is true, the reflection will be true, and the physical part will be perfect and

whole as the divine is always perfect and whole. Deepen the spiritualizing process in any part of the body, and the power of the spirit becomes supreme in that part. In consequence, adverse forces, diseased conditions and all wrongs, whatever their nature, will be removed in the same manner as darkness is removed by the light.

The body cannot be spiritualized through fasting, or through any form of self-denial; we cannot spiritualize the body by taking certain physical things away from the body, but by giving the body more and more of the spirit. And we give to the body of the spirit as we become more fully conscious of the spirit. Never deny the body anything that will add to the comfort, the beauty and the richness of physical existence. Take nothing away that is good in the without, but add more and more of that which is good in the within. Thus we increase the power of the spirit from within, and cause the personality to become a more perfect instrument through which the spirit may find expression.

When the interior life forces in any part of the body are changed, those physical conditions that may exist in that part are also changed; and any group of these forces will change the moment they are animated and permeated by the forces of the spirit. The power of the spirit lies deeper than and within the physical life; therefore, when the spiritual is unfolded, the physical will immediately begin to change to correspond with the nature of the spiritual. This is inevitable, because the spiritual is infinitely stronger than the physical. Any change from within will invariably produce a like change in the without; the realization of perfect health in the spirit must be followed by perfect health in the body, and the consciousness of greater spiritual strength will always bring greater physical strength. Any change from within will always be a change for the better; the spirit is absolutely good, therefore any change in the expression of the spirit will mean the expression of greater good. You cannot cause the spirit to express less; to act upon the spirit is to cause it to express more. When the spirit seems to express less, the reason is that we have clouded the mental mirror with "impressions of untruth," "mental pictures of imperfections" and other "foreign material" so that the light of the spirit is not properly reflected in the body. When we seem to be buried in materiality, sickness, adversity and distress, the reason is not that the spirit is dormant; the spirit never decreases in life, power and activity no matter what the person may do; but the perverted actions of the person will so confuse the mind that the life of the spirit will, for the time being, be hidden from conscious view. It is at such times that the soul seems to be lost, and that we seem to have lost all the light and all the truth we ever possessed; but the soul is never lost; it is the person that has strayed from the divine presence of the soul; let the person return to its own and we shall find the soul upon the divine throne of being as before, and we shall find again all the light and all the truth that we ever knew before. All that we have gathered of the good and the true is held in trust for us by the hand divine; and if we should lose our hold upon the true for a time we will not lose what was once our own; when we return to the fold we shall get everything back that we ever possessed. There is neither decrease nor loss in the spirit; in the life of the spirit it is always greater gain and continued increase; the limitless is the goal, and upward and onward forever is the path to that goal.

The higher consciousness ascends in the realization of the absolute, which is purely spiritual, the stronger becomes the spiritualizing process in the human system; and the stronger this process becomes, the greater becomes the supremacy of the spirit in human life. The entire human system is thus placed in the hands of the spirit, and wherever the spirit rules, in that place there is always health. Where the action of the spirit is strong, disease cannot possibly exist, and the action of the spirit invariably increases in every physical part where we clearly discern the spiritual counterpart. To more clearly discern this spiritual counterpart, train the mind to think of the spirit that is in everything whenever you think of anything. Let no action of mind cease with the mere recognition of the outer form; cause every mental action, every feeling and every thought to recognize the spirit, the soul and the greater life that is within the form. Gradually, but surely, consciousness will begin to act in the spiritual realm as well as in the physical realm; and whenever consciousness becomes active in the spiritual realm, the action of the spirit will increase in the field of that consciousness. Accordingly, whenever the consciousness of the spiritual is gained in any part of the body, the power of the spirit will rule in that part, and perfect health will be the result. The spiritual is always well; therefore, the physical becomes absolutely well the moment the spirit begins to reign.

All thought must be formed in the exact likeness of absolute truth. Whatever you think of, ask yourself what the absolute truth concerning that subject or object would naturally be. This will give the mind the tendency to face the brilliant light of supreme truth at all times, and every thought will be inspired by that light and formed in that light. The absolute truth is not a phase of truth or the truth about certain parts of being; it is the truth in the fullness of truth; it is complete in itself and lacks nothing that pertains to truth. Therefore, when all thought is formed in the likeness of absolute truth every thought will be complete in its own domain, and will express completeness wherever it may have the tendency to act. The expression of completeness means health, and it is thought that determines the nature of every expression that takes place in the human personality. Perfect health is never the result of a certain part of truth or of right thinking in any one of its phases. Perfect health can come only from absolute truth and from thinking that gives expression to absolute truth. To aim to think the truth in some of its phases while other phases are neglected is to confuse the mind and thus cloud the mental mirror so that the perfection of the real man is not properly reflected. The knowing of truth has nothing to do with phases of truth or parts of divine reality. To know the truth is to live in the allness of the spirit of truth and to realize that the perfection of being means the perfection of the whole of being. Perfect health is an inseparable part of absolute truth, and is gained only as the mind enters into the very life of absolute truth; that is, as the mind gains that position in spiritual consciousness where all things are discerned as reflections from the divine perfection of supreme reality. When this position is gained, all things are seen as they are—not as imperfections but as images of the divine, and to know that everything is as God is, is to know the absolute truth. It is this truth that gives freedom, because when the mind knows only the divinity of things it is not impressed with "thoughts of imperfection." The mental mirror is clear and clean, and the life, the health and the power of the divine man is perfectly reflected and expressed in the personal man —through and through every part of the personal man.

To place the mind completely in the consciousness of truth, it is necessary to realize distinctly what you are in the supreme state of your being. To know the truth, you must know the truth about yourself; and to enter the world of truth you must enter that real world in which you, yourself, have your true being. This world is the sphere of the "I Am;" in other words, that state of being wherein you become actually conscious of the great truth that "I Am" is identical with you. When you can clearly think of yourself as "I Am," and can actually feel that "I Am" is neither mind nor body, soul nor spirit, but is above all of these in the most supreme state of individualized being, you are beginning to enter within the sacred domains of absolute truth. Affirm as frequently as possible the statement, I AM THE REAL I AM, and try to realize, whenever you make that statement, that "I Am" is the reigning power in your being; that "I Am" is God individualized in your being; that "I Am" is the only begotten Son, the

Christ enthroned in your being; and that "I Am" actually is the "real you" of your being. You thus not only recognize the supreme position of "I Am," but you also recognize yourself as being "I Am;" you lift your consciousness of yourself out of "material thought" into the pure light of spiritual thought; you find your real self and you discover that you—the real you, the whole of you, reigns on high, where all life is forever in purity, health, power, freedom, truth; you become conscious of yourself in the world of supreme spiritual consciousness, and your eyes are opened in "another and a better world," to the great truth that you are, here and now, not only the likeness of God, but the individualized spirit of God. You find that the only difference between the "I Am" that is you and the "I Am That I Am," is that the former is individualized while the latter is infinite.

EPEND absolutely upon the Infinite for health, for life, for strength, for everything. Live consciously in God, and know that to be in God is to be in health, because God is absolute health. Whatever you proceed to do, act in conscious unity with God; enter so deeply into the spirit of every action that you can feel the life and the power of the Infinite in that action. You thus place yourself in the spirit of God, and everything that you do will be done in that spirit. Accordingly, everything that you think or do will give expression to the spirit; that which is in the spirit will, through your thinking and living, come forth into the person; external existence will give form to internal truth, and the same reality that you have become conscious of in the within will constitute the only real to you in the without. The imperfect or the adverse will no longer seem real to you; sickness and weakness will not be recognized as having tangible existence; in fact, they will not even be recognized as tangible conditions; only

that which is real will receive recognition at all, and the real is always well, always perfect, always true to the absolutely true. As you place yourself more and more in the spirit of God, such terms as "weakness," "evil," "sickness," and "wrong" will mean less and less to you; your mind will be so permeated with that truth that is everywhere present in the spirit of God that untruth can find no room in your consciousness. You will be so deeply and so constantly impressed with the conviction that you are always well that all thought of sickness will be foreign to your mind. You will discern so clearly that great truth that "all is good in God and all is in God," that beliefs about evil will not exist in your world whatever. When evil is mentioned you have "ears that hear not," because the word means nothing to you. In the truth there is no evil, and you are in the truth. You are in the spirit of God, and the spirit of God is truth, therefore you are in the truth. Being in the truth, you are, in like manner, unconscious of beliefs about sickness. You have no beliefs about sickness, and you never think of the word. Even when adverse conditions are felt in your body, you never think of sickness; you do not call such conditions sickness; you give them no name whatever; the name of God is sufficient upon such occasions, and in that name you invariably find peace.

To live in the truth is to mentally dwell upon the truth; that is, when we are in the spirit of truth the mind is completely absorbed in the truth; we are conscious of truth only; in consequence, we cannot be conscious of that which is not truth. It is therefore evident that when we pass into the spirit of truth we pass out of every condition that is not of the truth. We can, when we are in the spirit of truth, know nothing of sickness, weakness or pain. That which is wrong cannot enter the world of truth, but must be left behind when we enter the world of truth. And herein we find the path to complete emancipation. Whatever the conditions of the body may be, enter the spirit of truth and you are out of those conditions. Where you go, mind and body will go also; therefore, when you enter the truth, mind and body will also enter the truth, and will pass out of every condition that is not of the truth. You cannot be conscious of two opposite states at the same time; nor can you live in two separate and wholly dissimilar worlds at the same time; when you enter the world of truth, you must necessarily sever your consciousness completely from the world of untruth; when you are so completely in a state of perfect health that you are conscious of the very soul of health, you cannot possibly know anything about disease; and you do attain this supreme consciousness of health when you are in the truth, because no mind can enter completely into the truth without becoming absolutely conscious of all that is contained in the truth.

When the mind is absolutely conscious of any quality it becomes unconscious of everything that is outside of the world of that quality. To be conscious of the absolute is to be conscious of only that which is in the absolute; but such a consciousness does not narrow the mind or shut anything out from the mind, as many seem to think. The absolute contains everything that is real and true; therefore, when you enter absolute consciousness you lose your illusions only while you gain everything that real life has in store. When you enter completely into absolute consciousness you will forget sickness and evil; but those things we are more than willing to forget; and what is well to remember, as the number of people who have forgotten sickness increases, sickness in the world will decrease. When you blot out sickness and evil from your mind completely, you not only emancipate yourself but you will lessen the ills among scores, possibly hundreds and thousands. That we must think about disease, talk about disease and study disease in order to relieve mankind is not true. No one can ever know anything about sickness or evil. You cannot gain definite knowledge concerning empty space, nor can scientific facts be evolved from illusions. He who can completely forget all ills, is the greatest physician in the world.

The less you mention the ills of life the more you add to the comfort of life. He who gives no thought to the wrong must necessarily give all thought to the right; and he who gives his all to the right will perpetually increase the power of the right, not only in his own life, but in the life of the whole race. That which we think of we multiply; therefore, to forget the untrue is a great virtue; but we cannot forget the untrue unless we enter into the consciousness of that which is absolutely true. This, however, is not an attainment intercepted by difficulties; to be right is natural; to be wrong is unnatural; and to be natural is the easiest thing in the world.

To be absolutely conscious of the real and true, is to be true to the normal consciousness of the mind; therefore he who becomes unconscious of wrong, and completely forgets all wrong, is not taking some new or extraordinary step in mental action; he is simply using the mind the way nature intended that every mind should be used. The mind was not created for abnormal action, and to act upon evil, to dwell upon evil, to think about evil, to recognize evil—all of these are abnormal actions. The function of the mind is not to create thought that is out of harmony with truth, but to create thought in the likeness of truth. The purpose of thinking is to elevate the mind into higher states of consciousness, and it is only such thinking as takes absolute truth for its model that tends to rise in the scale.

Think of absolute consciousness as normal consciousness; realize that to be unconscious of sickness and evil is natural; remember the great truth that the more wrong you forget the more good you will gain, and that the less you know of pain the greater your power to relieve others of pain. This may seem absurd but the fact is that you know nothing of pain only when you have risen entirely above the world of pain; and when you have risen into that supreme state of being, you are in conscious possession of that power that is greater than anything that is in the world. You can conquer pain when you are above pain, and when you are above pain you are in that consciousness of true being where pain has no existence whatever, not even in your memory.

What you think of as normal will soon become a permanent state in your mind, providing it actually is normal in true being. Therefore, when you think of absolute consciousness as normal, such a consciousness will soon become a real factor in your mind. Then you may, whenever you like, become so absolutely conscious of perfect health that all ills will be forgotten completely. You may take mind and body so completely into the realization of truth that your entire being will entirely pass out of that which is contrary to truth. Then your emancipation will be complete, and you will be free indeed.

When you pray for health, do not simply ask for health. To continue to ask for health is to cause yourself to believe that you do not have health. But you are the image of God, and God is always well, therefore you are always well. You do not need health; you have, even now, absolute health; you do not have to ask for it; you already have it in abundance; believe that you have it, and you will realize its wholeness and power in every atom of your being. When you pray, enter into the spirit of God; feel that the spirit in you is the real in you, the all in you, and that the spirit in you is inseparable from the spirit in God. Then affirm with deep, spiritual conviction that you are in the truth what you wish to manifest; affirm that you possess in the real what you wish to possess in the actual. We should never separate the actual from the real in consciousness; the actual is that which appears; the real is that which forever is; but we should think of the two as one. They are one because the actual is always a reflection of the real. The real is the light; the actual is the coming forth of that light.

Think as God thinks, and God thinks only absolute truth. Live where God lives, and God lives only in the spirit of truth. To him who thinks the absolute truth, nothing is real but the world of absolute truth; and he gives conscious recognition only to that which is real. To live continually in the consciousness of the great truth that the real man is well, and that the real man is the whole man, is to think only health. What we are conscious of we think; and what appears in the personal man is the result of what we think of the real man. When every thought is created in the consciousness of health, every cell in the body will possess health. When the mind is full of health the body will be full of health, and every mind is full of health that is full of divine truth.

Sympathize only with the real, the true and the perfect. Select your mental companions from the world of truth only, and enter only those domains of thought that are illumined with the full light of the spirit. The absolute truth is not simply a remedy in the time of need; it is the very substance of life, and must be taken with every breath and with every thought as nourishment for true being. So long as human life is nourished with the truth, the human system will be actually filled with the power of truth; and there can be nothing less than perfect health—eternal health, where the truth reigns supremely.

HERE are moments when we know not where to turn; when all remedies fail, and all mortal aid seems vain. It is not only the hour of need, but the hour of the greatest need, and also the hour of the greatest pain. To know where to go when such moments come will be the most precious revelation that has ever been given to man. It has, however, been given ages ago, but those who had ears to hear, heard not.

There are many little things that can be done in every hour of need, and they are all of value; but the one thing above all things is usually neglected; and this one thing is GOING TO GOD. When we are in trouble we generally resort to all sorts of means before we go to Him. Instead of believing Him sufficient, we forget Him entirely, until the hour of utter despair. And for this reason, millions of sad events have transpired that could readily have been prevented.

Temporary means have their value, but only in proportion to the life and power from within with which they can act. When our consciousness of higher power is limited, external remedies may help for a time, and to a degree, but when this consciousness becomes so large that higher power is brought forth with might and main, temporary means become wholly unnecessary.

To realize that GOD IS SUFFICIENT, that His power can do all things, and that He is fully able to supply us, no matter how great may be the need—this is the great eternal rock upon which every life must establish its endless abiding place.

Though from this we are not to infer that to pray is the only thing to do in the hour of need; we may do everything that can minister in any way, but the first thing to do is to GO TO GOD and wholly depend upon Him. When we wholly depend upon Him, nothing further is required. He will prove Himself sufficient.

When your faith is not as strong as you wish it to be, use as many temporary means as you like, but remember that the higher life and power that you will receive by going to Him and depending upon Him—that is the remedy that will never fail. Do not trifle away your time with the lesser when you may receive the greater; and you invariably do receive the greater when you go to God first, depending absolutely upon Him.

Those who have not fully realized that God is sufficient, may, for some time, require temporary and external aid, and if they need this, let them have it by all means; no one must suffer, and whatever can relieve suffering, even but for a moment, should be used in faith. Besides, all things are from God, and all things contain, to a degree, His healing life. But things are limited in power and efficiency; therefore why should we continue to depend upon that which is small and uncertain, when we can go to God and receive from Him directly that which is limitless and faileth not?

When we grow in faith, we soon find ourselves in that beautiful state where difficult places are never met because His power and presence are ever with us to smoothen the pathway before us. And this high faith will come to everybody, who, in the hour of need, goes first to God, and depends wholly upon Him, regardless of what may come to pass.

These are the days of many changes in thoughts and methods; we are learning more of that unlimited power within us; and that this power can remove suffering and sickness of every description is being demonstrated daily; then why should we ever call upon external aid? To many, it seems wrong to employ material means when the greater spiritual remedies are always at hand; but in the presence of these conclusions, we often find that our prayers for healing are not answered, while external aid produces relief in many instances. And this fact is a problem that few seem able to solve.

The truth is, however, that power from on high comes to us according to our spiritual understanding and our nearness to God, therefore, while this understanding is undeveloped, we should not hesitate to seek temporary aid, if we think we need it; but the sooner we think that God is sufficient, the better. Because when we inwardly know that God is sufficient, He will prove Himself so to be.

When sickness or adversity threatens, remember, "I am thy God that healeth thee." Also, "I will never fail thee." And again, "Depend upon Me, I will not forsake thee or leave thee, I am thy Redeemer, I will care for thee." Full faith in these great statements will heal any one; and He will "raise thee up" from thy bed of sickness and threatening death, and "thou shalt be made whole" again and live.

When trouble comes, do not forget that "I am the Lord that brought thee out of Egypt." No matter how dense the darkness, how great the tribulations, or how hopeless the bondage, He can bring you out into the promised land of complete emancipation. It is a pleasure to God to take us away from our own self-created troubles, the only troubles we shall ever find, for the more we ask of God the more we please God; and He is sufficient, even in the hour of the very greatest need.

When we are in trouble we seldom think of God; we have lost faith in everything and everybody, and give up to fate. But this is the very moment when we should pray without ceasing, and consecrate every moment to the Most High. Go up into His presence when everything seems to go wrong; do not come down for a moment; keep your eye single upon Him, and think of nothing else. Have the faith that He is sufficient to cause everything to come right, and He will prove that He is sufficient. Ere long the clouds will break; the storm will pass away; and when the calm has come, we find that all things have worked together for good through every part of our recent experience.

Every person has frequently felt that he was not equal to the occasion; that he was losing ground and that failure seemed inevitable. He knew that a little more strength or reserve force, if he only had it, could carry him over the difficult places, and take him safely to the goal in view. But where may this added strength be received? At these moments, at this great hour of need, when our whole future seems to hang in the balance, we usually fail to remember that "they that wait upon the Lord shall renew their strength." Turn your heart and soul to the Infinite now, and you will receive at once that added power that can positively see you through.

Thousands of men and women have gone down in despair when the critical moment was at hand, when the time came that would determine whether loss or gain was to be their reward. But all of these people could have won a great and brilliant career by going to God in the hour of need and receiving from Him the power required to carry them through. God is sufficient; and it matters not how dark the day may be or how hopeless the goal in view; call upon Him for new power and He will raise you up unto victory.

There is possibly no hour that is more dreary than the one that comes when every friend seems to be lost; when we have no one to whom we can speak heart to heart. The whole universe seems empty and every moment an eternity of suspense. But at this hour of great need there is someone that is not far away, someone who can take away the burden, and relieve the heart of every sorrow and pain. This Great Friend may have been forgotten, nevertheless He is ever at hand, and ever sufficient; the very best friend of all, for "I am with you always, even unto the end of the world."

When we go to Him and open our hearts to His tenderness and love; not a mere sentimental experience, but a real meeting face to face with the friend of all souls; when we do this, we become so filled with real love and sympathy that the very best of human friends will be drawn to us in large numbers. By seeking the friend of all friends, we receive His divine friendship, and in addition all the human friendship that we can possibly desire.

When we seem to be lost in bondage, mistakes and wrong, so we cannot find

a single ray of light anywhere, we are
not required to fall down upon our knees,
and in agonizing petitions implore the
mercy and forgiveness of the Supreme.
Neither need we be afraid that we are
lost, or that we have to pass through
ages of darkness and sin. No, such
thoughts are wrong, for wherever we
may be, there God will be also; and
whatever our condition may be, He is
always sufficient. Do we believe this
with the whole heart? Do we realize
that the Infinite can, in one short moment, take us out completely from all
the bondage and wrong in the world?
Do we live in the conviction that He is
sufficient no matter what may happen
to us in the present or in the future?
These are great thoughts to think of, for
the moment we seek emancipation
through Him, our days in bondage are
numbered. The storm will soon be over;
then will come the beautiful calm and
the sun will shine again.

We make entirely too much of the adverse conditions we meet, and by giving
so much thought to the threatening ills,
we not only aggravate these ills, but we
forget that "God shall wipe away all
tears from their eyes." To live in this

faith is to so live that tears will never come any more.

We all realize that the hour of need is usually the critical moment, and what we do at this hour nearly always determines what experiences we are to meet for days and even years to come. Therefore, we cannot give this hour too much right thought; we cannot use it with too much care and wisdom. But if the hour of need, "the hour of man's extremity and God's opportunity," is to become the turning point to greater things, we must call upon God and seek His guidance and power directly. No matter what other things we may do, His power and presence must be sought first. His help is the greatest of all, and with Him all things are possible. In the hour of need GO TO GOD first; depend upon Him, for He is sufficient.

HE mind that would heal the sick must develop faith, love, soul-serenity and spiritual consciousness. His faith must be that faith that can go out upon the seeming void and always find the solid rock; his love must be that love that loves everything at all times, and from the heart, because it IS love; the calmness of his soul must be so deep, and so high, that he can truthfully say at any time "None of these things move me;" and his consciousness of the spiritual must be so perfect that he INWARDLY KNOWS that man is divine, created in the exact image and likeness of God.

However, these four essentials do not constitute the real power that heals; they simply awaken the real power, and are therefore efficient only as far as they are orderly combined with the desired object in view. The real power in healing is the coming forth of the spirit, the soul expressing itself through the body, the Word becoming flesh.

When any mind can awaken the spiritual life in others, he can heal others; and every person can heal himself who can awaken spirituality in himself.

The spirit is perfect and whole in every manner; and the power of the spirit is greater than any force or condition that can possibly exist in the body; therefore, when the power of the spirit enters the body, every part of the body will be permeated through and through with health, wholeness and life; and so strong will be the force of this wholesome life from within that all sickness, weakness or disorder will have to take flight.

When the spiritual nature of man is awakened, we turn on, so to speak, the light of his divine life, and as this divine life is health, absolute and invincible, the darkness of disease or disorder must disappear. But this divine life is not simply unconquerable health; it is everything that is perfect and true in the spiritual being of man; it is that universal light that eliminates all darkness; therefore, to awaken man's spiritual nature is to secure emancipation from everything that is adverse in human existence.

The spiritual nature of man is created in the likeness of God; it is as God is, and as God can neither be sick, weak nor out of order in any manner whatever, the spiritual nature of man cannot be sick, weak nor out of order. In brief, when the spiritual nature of man is awakened, he will express the likeness of God in everything. His body will be perfectly well, his mind will be sweet and wholesome, his character will be strong and beautiful, and his soul will live on the heights.

There are no imperfect conditions in mind or body that will not disappear, gradually or rapidly, as the spiritual life is awakened. "Greater is He that is in you than he that is in the world." It is the one only direct method of healing, while all other methods are indirect.

Indirect methods, whether mental or physical, do not always heal; usually they simply produce a temporary relief; but the one great direct method removes cause and effect and all; it brings forth a new life from the strong, wholesome, spotless within, therefore every trace of the old life, with its adverse conditions, must vanish absolutely.

To live perpetually in the spiritual attitude is to retain perpetual health because there can be no disease in that which is spiritual, and so long as the mind is in a spiritual attitude the body will be in a spiritual condition.

When the body is in a spiritual condition it is immune from every disease, including all forms of contagious diseases; it is in that state where health is so strong and so positive that the negative actions of disease are simply powerless in its presence.

The chemical elements of a spiritualized body are sustained in the very life of the spirit, and the health of the spirit is unconquerable; nothing from without can disturb it. Its power comes from the Supreme Power and that power is irresistible, invincible and immovable. It is what it is, and nothing can cause it to be different.

To place the body in the condition of that health from within that is so strong that nothing can cause it to be anything else but health, is to secure complete immunity from all ills, and the body will be in this condition so long as the mind lives in the spirit; that is, in the spiritual understanding of its own divinity.

This spiritual understanding develops with the development of real spirituality and the awakening of more and more of the sublime spiritual life, and as this development continues, the power of health, wholeness and harmony will increase accordingly.

And he said unto her, Daughter, thy faith hath made thee whole.—Mark 5:34.

HIS is the woman who had suffered many things from many physicians, and there are thousands today with a similar experience; but these thousands can all be healed, every one. Faith can do all things, and we all can have faith. This woman was healed by simply touching the hem of His garment; we can be healed in the same way. The Christ is here today; the presence of his spirit is within us and all about us; we may at any time touch the hem of His garment and feel that we are filled with His power through and through. Then we shall, as this woman did, feel in our bodies that we are healed; the adverse condition is dried up, withered away, vanished completely, and we are every whit clean and strong.

This is the inner workings of faith; when we inwardly feel that we are healed, we ARE healed; whatsoever we inwardly feel, believing, that shall surely come to pass. Faith is not of the letter, but of the spirit; when we have faith we enter into the inner life of the spirit, and the power of that life can do and will do whatever we believe it can do. When we have faith we do not depend upon the outer, but upon the inner, and we thereby place ourselves in touch with the inner; we actually enter into the interior life and are therefore filled through and through with the supreme spirit of that life.

The spiritual life is always perfectly whole; when we have faith we enter into the spiritual life; and as we are no longer in darkness when we enter the light, we are no longer in sickness when we enter absolute spiritual health. When we are in the spirit, we inwardly feel that we are in health, strength and wholeness, and what we inwardly feel is true; it will come to pass; it is now coming to pass. The moment we feel health and strength in the spirit of the body, health and strength will begin to come forth; the turn for the better will come that very hour; if our faith is strong we shall be restored instantaneously, but in any event we will be made every whit whole.

To have the perfect faith and place in action the full power of faith, it is necessary to enter into the soul of faith; that is, the mind should recognize that interior spiritual power that animates the action of faith, and as we consciously come into perfect touch with this power, we INWARDLY FEEL the presence of this power. Then whatsoever we desire that power to do, believing, the same shall be done. "And all things, whatsoever ye shall ask in prayer, believing, ye shall receive."

When this woman touched the hem of His garment, Jesus "perceived in himself that the power proceeding from Him had gone forth." Through her deep, strong faith, she placed herself in touch with the spiritual power that was so immensely strong in the divine personality of Jesus Christ; and as this power entered her being she "felt in her body" that she was whole. Her faith opened the way and placed her life in conscious touch with Supreme life; the power of the spirit proceeding from the Christ gave her wholeness and freedom.

But the same Christ is here today. The Christ is enthroned in every soul; by entering into the pure spiritual life of the soul we may touch the hem of His garment now, and the same power proceeding from the Christ shall come forth into us; then we shall also "feel in the body" that we are whole. Our faith has opened the way; we are in Him and He in us, and all is well.